# Stronger
## ~ in the ~
# Broken
# Places

# Max Lucado

**WORD PUBLISHING**
Dallas · London · Vancouver · Melbourne

**Stronger in the Broken Places**
published by Word Publishing

© 1994 by Max Lucado

"Get Rid of Regret", "Dealing with Anger",
"The Foundation of Faith", and "Overcoming Your Heritage"
are taken from *When God Whispers Your Name* © 1994 by Max Lucado

Unless otherwise indicated, all Scripture references are from
the New Century Version of the Bible, copyright © 1987, 1988,
1991, Word Publishing.
ISBN 0-8499-5103-8
Printed in the United States of America

## *Stronger in the Broken Places*
· · · · · · ·

*Resentment . . . a door quietly closes.*

*Anger . . . the door slams shut!*

*Hurts from your heritage . . . fasten the latch!*

*Weakened faith . . . throw the bolt!*

F*our elements that can lock up a heart, keeping delight out and darkness in. Resentment, the cocaine of the emotions. Anger, the destroyer of joy. Your heritage—the straitjacket of expectation. Declining faith—the marauder of hope.*

*And four keys to unlocking the heart . . . to replacing resentment with forgiveness, anger with understanding . . . to repairing the past with the possible . . . to rediscovering faith.*

## Chapter One

. . . . . .

# Get Rid of Regret

Y OU HAVE one. A sack. A burlap sack. Probably aren't aware of it, may not have been told about it. Could be you don't remember it. But it was given to you. A sack. An itchy, scratchy burlap sack.

You needed the sack so you could carry the stones. Rocks, boulders, pebbles. All sizes. All shapes. All unwanted.

You didn't request them. You didn't seek them. But you were given them.

Don't remember?

Some were rocks of rejection. You were given one the time you didn't pass the tryout. It wasn't for lack of effort. Heaven only knows how much you practiced. You thought you were good enough for the team. But the coach didn't. The instructor didn't. You thought you were good enough, but they said you weren't.

They and how many others?

You don't have to live long before you get a collection of stones. Make a poor grade. Make a bad choice. Make a mess. Get called a few names. Get mocked. Get abused.

And the stones don't stop with adolescence. I sent a letter this week to an unemployed man who's been rejected in more than fifty interviews.

And so the sack gets heavy. Heavy with stones. Stones of rejection. Stones we don't deserve.

Along with a few we do.

4

Look into the burlap sack and you see that not all the stones are from rejections. There is a second type of stone. The stone of regret.

Regret for the time you lost your temper.

Regret for the day you lost control.

Regret for the moment you lost your pride.

Regret for the years you lost your priorities.

And even regret for the hour you lost your innocence.

One stone after another, one guilty stone after another.

With time the sack gets heavy. We get tired. How can you have dreams for the future when all your energy is required to shoulder the past?

No wonder some people look miserable. The sack slows the step. The sack chafes. Helps explain the irritation on so many faces, the sag in so many steps, the drag in so many shoulders, and most of all, the desperation in so many acts.

You're consumed with doing whatever it takes to get some rest.

So you take the sack to the office. You resolve to work so hard you'll forget about the sack. You arrive early and stay late. People are impressed. But when it's time to go home, there is the sack—waiting to be carried out.

You carry the stones into happy hour. With a name like that, it must bring relief. So you set the sack on the floor, sit on the stool, and drink a few. The music gets loud and your head gets light. But then it's time to go and you look down and there is the sack.

You drag it into therapy. You sit on the couch with the sack at your feet and spill all your stones on the floor and name them one by one. The therapist listens. She empathizes. Some helpful counsel is given. But when the time is up, you're obliged to gather the rocks and take them with you.

You get so desperate you try a weekend rendezvous. A little excitement. A risky embrace. A night of stolen passion. And for a moment the load is lighter. But then the weekend passes. Sunday's sun sets and awaiting you on Monday's doorstep is—you got it—your sack of regrets and rejections.

Some even take the sack to church. Perhaps religion will help, we reason. But instead of removing a few stones, some well-meaning but misguided preacher may add to the load. God's messengers sometimes give more hurt than help. And you might leave the church with a few new rocks in your sack.

The result? A person slugging his way through life, weighed down by the past. I don't know if you've noticed, but it's hard to be thoughtful when you're carrying a burlap sack. It's hard to be affirming when you are affirmation-starved. It's hard to be forgiving when you feel guilty.

Paul had an interesting observation about the way we treat people. He said it about marriage, but the principle applies in any relationship. "The man who loves his wife loves himself" (Eph. 5:28). There is a correlation between the way you feel about yourself and the way you feel about others. If you are at peace with yourself—if you like yourself—you will get along with others.

The converse is also true. If you don't like yourself, if you are ashamed, embarrassed, or angry, other people are going to know it. The tragic part of the burlap-sack story is we tend to throw our stones at those we love.

Unless the cycle is interrupted.

Which takes us to the question, "How *does* a person get relief?"

Which, in turn, takes us to one of the kindest verses in the Bible, "Come to me, all of you who are tired and have heavy loads, and I will give you rest. Accept my teachings and learn from me, because I am gentle and humble in spirit, and you will find rest for your lives. The teaching I ask you to accept is easy; the load I give you to carry is light" (Matt. 11:28–30).

You knew I was going to say that. I can see you holding this book and shaking your head. "I've tried that. I've read the Bible, I've sat on the pew—but I've never received relief."

If that is the case, could I ask a delicate but deliberate question? Could it be that you went to religion and didn't go to God? Could it be that you went to a church, but never saw Christ?

"Come to me," the verse reads.

It's easy to go to the wrong place. I did yesterday. I was in Portland, Maine, catching a flight to Boston. Went to the desk, checked my bag, got my ticket, and went to the gate. I went past security, took my seat, and waited for the flight to be called. I waited and waited and waited—finally, I went up to the desk to ask the attendant and she looked at me and said, "You're at the wrong gate."

Now, what if I'd pouted and sighed, "Well, there must not be a flight to Boston. Looks like I'm stuck."

You would have said to me, "You're not stuck. You're just at the wrong gate. Go down to the right gate and try again."

It's not that you haven't tried—you've tried for years to deal with your past. Alcohol. Affairs. Workaholism. Religion.

Jesus says He is the solution for weariness of soul.

## Chapter Two

· · · · · · ·

# Dealing with Anger

**F**ORGIVE ME if this chapter is disjointed. As I write, I am angry. I am angered by a cricket. He's loud. He's obnoxious. He's hidden. And he's in big trouble if I ever find him.

I arrived at my office early. Two hours before my alarm sounded, I was here. Sleeves rolled back and computer humming. *Beat the phones*, I thought. *Get a jump on the morning*, I planned. *Get a leg up on the day*.

But *Get your hands on that cricket* is what I keep mumbling.

Now, I have nothing against nature. The melody of a canary, I love. The pleasant hum of the wind in the leaves, I relish. But the predawn *raack-raack-raack* of a cricket bugs me.

So I get on my knees and follow the sound through the office. I peek under boxes. I pull books off the shelves. I get on my belly and look under my desk. Humbling. I've been sabotaged by a one-inch bug.

What is this insolent irritant that reduces a man to bug-stalker?

Finally, I isolate the culprit.

Rats, he's behind a shelf. Out of my reach. Hidden in a haven of plywood. I can't get to him. All I can do is throw pens at the base of the shelf. So I do. *Pop. Pop. Pop.* One after another. A barrage of Bics. He finally shuts up.

But the silence lasts only a minute.

So forgive me if my thoughts are fragmented, but I'm launching artillery every other paragraph. This is no way to work. This is no way to start the day. My floor is cluttered. My pants are dirty. My train of thought is derailed. I mean, how can you write about anger with a stupid bug in your office?

Oooops. Guess I'm in the right frame of mind after all . . .

*Anger.* This morning it's easy to define: the noise of the soul. *Anger.* The unseen irritant of the heart. *Anger.* The relentless invader of silence.

Just like the cricket, anger irritates.

Just like the cricket, anger isn't easily silenced.

Just like the cricket, anger has a way of increasing in volume until it's the only sound we hear. The louder it gets the more desperate we become.

When we are mistreated, our animalistic response is to go on the hunt. Instinctively, we double up our fists. Getting even is only natural. Which, incidentally, is precisely the problem. Revenge is natural, not spiritual. Getting even is the rule of the jungle. Giving grace is the rule of the kingdom.

Some of you are thinking, *Easy for you to say, Max, sitting there in your office with a cricket as your chief irritant. You ought to try living with my wife.* Or, *You ought to have to cope with my past.*

Or, *You ought to raise my kids. You don't know how my ex has mistreated me. You don't have any idea how hard my life has been.*

And you're right, I don't. But I have a very clear idea how miserable your future will be unless you deal with your anger.

X-ray the soul of the vengeful and behold the tumor of bitterness: black, menacing, malignant. Carcinoma of the spirit. Its fatal fibers creep around the edge of the heart and ravage it. Yesterday you can't alter, but your reaction to yesterday you can. The past you cannot change, but your response to your past you can.

Impossible, you say? Let me try to show you otherwise.

Imagine you are from a large family—a dozen or so kids. A family more blended than the Brady bunch. All the children are from the same dad, but they have four or five different moms.

Imagine also that your dad is a sneak and has been one for a long time. Everybody knows it. Everybody knows he cheated your uncle out of the estate. Everybody knows he ran like a coward to avoid getting caught.

Let's also imagine that your great-uncle tricked your dad into marrying your mother's sister. He got your dad drunk before the wedding and had his ugly daughter go to the altar instead of the pretty one your dad thought he was marrying.

That didn't slow down your father, though. He just married them both. The one he loved couldn't have kids, so he slept with her maid. In fact, he had a habit of sleeping with most of the kitchen help; as a result, most of your siblings resemble the cooks.

Finally the bride your dad wanted to marry in the first place gets pregnant . . . and you are born.

You're the favored son . . . and your brothers know it.

You get a car. They don't. You get Armani; they get K-Mart. You get summer camp; they get summer jobs. You get educated; they get angry.

And they get even. They sell you to some foreign service project, put you on a plane for Egypt, and tell your dad you got shot by a sniper. You find yourself surrounded by people you don't know, learning a language you don't understand, and living in a culture you've never seen.

Imaginary tale? No. It's the story of Joseph. A favored son in a bizarre family, he had every reason to be angry.

He tried to make the best of it. He became the chief servant of the head of the Secret Service. His boss's wife tried to seduce him, and when he refused, she pouted and he ended up in prison. Pharaoh got wind of the fact that Joseph could interpret dreams and let him take a shot at some of Pharaoh's own.

When Joseph interpreted them he got promoted out of the prison into the palace as prime minister. The second highest position in all of Egypt. The only person Joseph bowed before was the king.

Meanwhile a famine hits and Jacob, Joseph's father, sends his sons to Egypt for a foreign loan. The brothers don't know it, but they are standing in front of the same brother they sold to the Gypsies some twenty-two years earlier.

They don't recognize Joseph, but Joseph recognizes them. A bit balder and paunchier, but they are the same brothers. Imagine Joseph's thoughts. The last time he saw these faces, he was looking up at them from the bottom of a pit. The last time he heard these voices, they were laughing at him. The last time they called his name, they called him every name in the book.

Now is his chance to get even. He has complete control. One snap of his fingers and these brothers are dead. Better yet, slap some manacles on their hands and feet and let them see what an Egyptian dungeon is like. Let them sleep in the mud. Let them mop floors. Let them learn Egyptian.

Revenge is within Joseph's power. And there is power in revenge. Intoxicating power.

Haven't we tasted it? Haven't we been tempted to get even?

As we escort the offender into the court-room, we announce, "He hurt me!" The jurors shake their heads in disgust. "He abandoned me!" we explain, and the chambers echo with our accusation. "Guilty!" the judge snarls as he slams the gavel. "Guilty!" the jury agrees. "Guilty!" the audience proclaims. We delight in this moment of justice. We relish this pound of flesh. So we prolong the event. We tell the story again and again and again.

Now let's freeze-frame that scene. I have a question. Not for all of you, but for a few of you. Some of you are in the courtroom. The courtroom of complaint. Some of you are rehashing the same hurt every chance you get with anyone who will listen.

For you, I have this question: Who made you God? I don't mean to be cocky, but why are you doing his work for Him?

"Vengeance is Mine," God declared. "I will repay" (Heb. 10:30 NKJV).

"Don't say, 'I'll pay you back for the wrong you did.' Wait for the Lord, and he will make things right" (Prov. 20:22).

Judgment is God's job. To assume otherwise is to assume God can't do it.

Revenge is irreverent. When we strike back we are saying, "I know vengeance is Yours, God, but I just didn't think You'd punish enough. I thought I'd better take this situation into my own hands. You have a tendency to be a little soft."

Joseph understands that. Rather than get even, he reveals his identity and has his father and the rest of the family brought to Egypt. He grants them safety and provides them a place to live. They live in harmony for seventeen years.

But then Jacob dies and the moment of truth comes. The brothers have a hunch that with Jacob gone they'll be lucky to get out of Egypt with their heads on their shoulders. So they go to Joseph and plead for mercy.

"Your father gave this command before he died. . . . 'Tell Joseph to forgive you'" (Gen. 50:16–17). (I have to smile at the thought of grown men talking like this. Don't they sound like kids, whining, "Daddy said to be nice to us"?)

Joseph's response? "When Joseph received the message, he cried" (Gen. 50:17). *"What more do I have to do?"* his tears implore. *"I've given you a home. I've provided for your families. Why do you still mistrust my grace?"*

Please read carefully the two statements he makes to his brothers. First he asks, "Can I do what only God can do?" (v. 19).

May I restate the obvious? Revenge belongs to God! If vengeance is God's, then it is not ours. God has not asked us to settle the score or get even. Ever.

Why? The answer is found in the second part of Joseph's statement: "You meant to hurt me, but God turned your evil into good to save the lives of many people, which is being done" (v. 20).

Forgiveness comes easier with a wide-angle lens. Joseph uses one to get the whole picture. He refuses to focus on the betrayal of his brothers without also seeing the loyalty of his God.

It always helps to see the big picture.

Some time ago I was in an airport lobby when I saw an acquaintance enter. He was a man I hadn't seen in a while but had thought about often. He'd been through a divorce, and I was close enough to it to know that he deserved some of the blame.

I noticed he was not alone. Beside him was a woman. *Why, that scoundrel! Just a few months out and here he has another lady?*

Any thought of greeting him disappeared as I passed judgment on his character. But then he saw me. He waved at me. He motioned me over. I was caught. I was trapped. I'd have to go visit with the reprobate. So I did.

"Max, meet my aunt and her husband."

I gulped. I hadn't noticed the man.

"We're on our way to a family reunion. I know they would really like to meet you."

"We use your books in our home Bible study," my friend's uncle spoke up. "You've got some great insights."

"If only you knew," I said to myself. I had committed a common sin of the unforgiving. I had cast a vote without knowing the story.

To forgive someone is to admit our limitations. We've been given only one piece of life's jigsaw puzzle. Only God has the cover of the box.

To forgive someone is to display reverence. Forgiveness is not saying the one who hurt you was right. Forgiveness is stating that God is fair and He will do what is right.

After all, don't we have enough things to do without trying to do God's work too?

Guess what. I just noticed something. The cricket is quiet. I got so wrapped up in this chapter I forgot him. I haven't thrown a pen for an hour. Guess he fell asleep. Could be that's what he wanted to do all along, but I kept waking him up with my Bics.

He ended up getting some rest. I ended up finishing this chapter. Remarkable what gets accomplished when we let go of our anger.

# The Foundation of Faith

I STAND six steps from the bed's edge. My arms extended. Hands open. On the bed Sara—all four years of her—crouches, posed like a playful kitten. She's going to jump. But she's not ready. I'm too close.

"Back more, Daddy," she stands and dares.

I dramatically comply, confessing admiration for her courage. After two giant steps I stop. "More?" I ask.

"Yes!" Sara squeals, hopping on the bed.

With each step she laughs and claps and motions for more. When I'm on the other side of the canyon, when I'm beyond the reach of mortal man, when I am but a tiny figure on the horizon, she stops me. "There, stop there."

"Are you sure?"

"I'm sure," she shouts. I extend my arms. Once again she crouches, then springs. Superman without a cape. Skydiver without a chute. Only her heart flies higher than her body. In that airborne instant her only hope is her father. If he proves weak, she'll fall. If he proves cruel, she'll crash. If he proves forgetful, she'll tumble to the hard floor.

But such fear she does not know, for her father she does. She trusts him. Four years under the same roof have convinced her he is reliable. He is not superhuman, but he is strong. He is not holy, but he is good. He's not brilliant, but he doesn't have to be to remember to catch his child when she jumps.

And so she flies.

And so she soars.

And so he catches her and the two rejoice at the wedding of her trust and his faithfulness.

∞

I stand a few feet from another bed. This time no one laughs. The room is solemn. A machine pumps air into a tired body. A monitor metronomes the beats of a weary heart. The woman on the bed is no child. She was, once. Decades back. She was. But not now.

Like Sara, she must trust. Only days out of the operating room, she's just been told she'll have to return. Her frail hand squeezes mine. Her eyes mist with fear.

Unlike Sara, she sees no father. But the Father sees her. *Trust him,* I say to us both. Trust the voice that whispers your name. Trust the hands to catch.

∞

I sit across the table from a good man. Good and afraid. His fear is honest. Stocks are down. Inflation is up. He has payroll to meet and bills to pay. He hasn't squandered or gambled or played. He has worked hard and prayed often, but now he's afraid. Beneath the flannel suit lies a timid heart.

He stirs his coffee and stares at me with the eyes of Wile E. Coyote who just realizes he's run beyond the edge of a cliff. He's about to fall and fall fast. He's Peter on the water, seeing the storm and not the face. He's Peter in the waves, hearing the wind and not the voice.

*Trust*, I urge. But the word thuds. He's unaccustomed to such strangeness. He's a man of reason. Even when the kite flies beyond the clouds he still holds the string. But now the string has slipped. And the sky is silent.

∞

I stand a few feet from a mirror and see the face of a man who failed . . . who failed his Maker. Again. I promised I wouldn't, but I did. I was quiet when I should have been bold. I took a seat when I should have taken a stand.

If this were the first time, it would be different. But it isn't. How many times can one fall and expect to be caught?

*Trust.* Why is it easy to tell others and so hard to remind self? Can God deal with death? I told the woman so. Can God deal with debt? I ventured as much with the man. Can God hear yet one more confession from these lips?

The face in the mirror asks.

∞

I sit a few feet from a man on death row. Jewish by birth. Tentmaker by trade. Apostle by calling. His days are marked. I'm curious about what bolsters this man as he nears his execution. So I ask some questions.

Do you have family, Paul? *I have none.*

What about your health? *My body is beaten and tired.*

What do you own? *I have my parchments. My pen. A cloak.*

And your reputation? *Well, it's not much. I'm a heretic to some, a maverick to others.*

Do you have friends? *I do, but even some of them have turned back.*

Any awards? *Not on earth.*

Then what do you have, Paul? No belongings. No family. Criticized by some. Mocked by others. What do you have, Paul? What do you have that matters?

I sit back quietly and watch. Paul rolls his hand into a fist. He looks at it. I look at it. What is he holding? What does he have?

He extends his hand so I can see. As I lean forward, he opens his fingers. I peer at his palm. It's empty.

*I have my faith. It's all I have. But it's all I need. I have kept the faith.*

Paul leans back against the wall of his cell and smiles. And I lean back against another and stare into the face of a man who has learned that there is more to life than meets the eye.

For that's what faith is. Faith is trusting what the eye can't see.

Eyes see the prowling lion. Faith sees Daniel's angel.

Eyes see storms. Faith sees Noah's rainbow.

Eyes see giants. Faith sees Canaan.

Your eyes see your faults. Your faith sees your Savior.

Your eyes see your guilt. Your faith sees His blood.

Your eyes see your grave. Your faith sees a city whose Builder and Maker is God.

Your eyes look in the mirror and see a sinner, a failure, a promise-breaker. But by faith you look in the mirror and see a robed prodigal bearing the ring of grace on your finger and the kiss of your Father on your face.

But wait a minute, someone asks. How do I know this is true? Nice prose, but give me the facts. How do I know these aren't just fanciful hopes?

Part of the answer can be found in Sara's little leaps of faith. Her older sister, Andrea, was in the room watching, and I asked Sara if she would jump to Andrea. Sara refused. I tried to convince her. She wouldn't budge. "Why not?" I asked.

"I only jump to big arms."

If we think the arms are weak, we won't jump.

For that reason, the Father flexed His muscles. "God's power is very great for those who believe," Paul taught. "That power is the same as the great strength God used to raise Christ from the dead" (Eph. 1:19–20).

Next time you wonder if God can catch you, read that verse. The very arms that defeated death are the arms awaiting you.

Next time you wonder if God can forgive you, read that verse. The very hands that were nailed to the cross are open for you.

And the next time you wonder if you will survive the jump, think of Sara and me. If a flesh-and-bone-headed dad like me can catch his child, don't you think your eternal Father can catch you?

*Chapter Four*

· · · · · · ·

# Overcoming Your Heritage

S TEFAN CAN TELL you about family trees. He makes his living from them. He inherited a German forest that has been in his family for 400 years. The trees he harvests were planted 180 years ago by his great-grandfather. The trees he plants won't be ready for market until his great-grandchildren are born.

He's part of a chain.

"Every generation must make a choice," he told me. "They can either pillage or plant. They can rape the landscape and get rich, or they can care for the landscape, harvest only what is theirs, and leave an investment for their children."

Stefan harvests seeds sown by men he never knew.

Stefan sows seeds to be harvested by descendants he'll never see.

Dependent upon the past, responsible for the future: he's part of a chain.

Like us. Children of the past, are we. Parents of the future. Heirs. Benefactors. Recipients of the work done by those before. Born into a forest we didn't seed.

Which leads me to ask, how's your forest?

As you stand on the land bequeathed by your ancestors, how does it look? How do you feel?

Pride at legacy left? Perhaps. Some inherit nourished soil. Deeply rooted trees of conviction. Row after row of truth and heritage. Could be that you stand in the forest of your fathers with pride. If so, give thanks, for many don't.

Many aren't proud of their family trees. Poverty. Shame. Abuse. Such are the forests found by some of you. The land was pillaged. Harvest was taken, but no seed was sown.

Perhaps you were reared in a home of bigotry and so you are intolerant of minorities. Perhaps you were reared in a home of greed, hence your desires for possessions are insatiable.

Perhaps your childhood memories bring more hurt than inspiration. The voices of your past cursed you, belittled you, ignored you. At the time, you thought such treatment was typical. Now you see it isn't.

And now you find yourself trying to explain your past.

I came across a story of a man who must have had such thoughts. His heritage was tragic. His grandfather was a murderer and a mystic who sacrificed his own children in ritual abuse. His dad was a punk who ravaged houses of worship and made a mockery of believers. He was killed at the age of twenty-four . . . by his friends.

The men were typical of their era. They lived in a time when prostitutes purveyed their wares in houses of worship. Wizards treated disease with chants. People worshiped stars and followed horoscopes. More thought went into superstition and voodoo than into the education of the children.

It was a dark time in which to be born. What do you do when your grandfather followed black magic, your father was a scoundrel, and your nation is corrupt?

Follow suit? Some assumed he would. Branded him as a delinquent before he was born, a chip off the old rotten block. You can almost hear the people moan as he passes, "Gonna be just like his dad."

But they were wrong. He wasn't. He reversed the trend. He defied the odds. He stood like a dam against the trends of his day and rerouted the future of his nation. His achievements were so remarkable, we still tell his story twenty-six hundred years later.

The story of King Josiah. The world has seen wiser kings; the world has seen wealthier kings; the world has seen more powerful kings. But history has never seen a more courageous king than young Josiah.

Born some six hundred years before Jesus, Josiah inherited a fragile throne and a tarnished crown. The temple was in disarray, the Law was lost, and the people worshiped whatever god they desired. But by the end of Josiah's thirty-one-year reign, the temple had been rebuilt, the idols destroyed, and the law of God was once again elevated to a place of prominence and power.

The forest had been reclaimed.

Josiah's grandfather, King Manasseh, was remembered as the king who filled "Jerusalem from one end to the other with [the people's] blood" (2 Kings 21:16). His father, King Amon, died at the hands of his own officers. "He did what God said was wrong," reads his epitaph.

The citizens formed a posse and killed the assassins, and eight-year-old Josiah ascended the throne. Early in his reign Josiah made a brave choice. "He lived as his ancestor David had lived, and he did not stop doing what was right" (2 Kings 22:2).

He flipped through his family scrapbook until he found an ancestor worthy of emulation. Josiah skipped his dad's life and bypassed his grandpa's. He leapfrogged back in time until he found David and resolved, "I'm going to be like him."

The principle? We can't choose our parents, but we can choose our mentors.

And since Josiah chose David (who had chosen God), things began to happen.

The people tore down the altars for the Baal gods as Josiah directed.

Josiah cut down the incense altars.

Josiah . . . broke up the Asherah idols and . . . beat them into powder.

He burned the bones of the priests.

Josiah broke down the altars.

He cut down all the incense altars in all of Israel. (2 Chron. 34:4–5, 7)

Not what you call a public relations tour. But, then again, Josiah was not out to make friends. He was out to make a statement: "What my fathers taught, I don't teach. What they embraced, I reject."

And he wasn't finished. Four years later, at the age of twenty-six, he turned his attention to the temple. It was in shambles. The people had allowed it to fall into disrepair. But Josiah was determined. Something had happened that fueled his passion to restore the temple. A baton had been passed. A torch had been received.

Early in his reign he'd resolved to serve the God of his ancestor David. Now he chose to serve the God of someone else. Note 2 Chronicles 34:8: "In Josiah's eighteenth year as king, he made Judah and the Temple pure again. He sent Shaphan . . . to repair the Temple of the Lord, *the God of Josiah*" (emphasis mine).

God was *his* God. David's faith was Josiah's faith. He had found the God of David and made Him his own. As the temple was being rebuilt, one of the workers happened upon a scroll. On the scroll were the words of God given to Moses nearly a thousand years earlier.

When Josiah heard the words, he was shocked. He wept that his people had drifted so far from God that His Word was not a part of their lives.

He sent word to a prophetess and asked her, "What will become of our people?"

She told Josiah that since he had repented when he heard the words, his nation would be spared the anger of God (see 2 Chron. 34:27). Incredible. An entire generation received grace because of the integrity of one man.

Could it be that God placed him on earth for that reason?

Could it be that God has placed you on earth for the same?

Maybe your past isn't much to brag about. Maybe you've seen raw evil. And now you, like Josiah, have to make a choice. Do you rise above the past and make a difference? Or do you remain controlled by the past and make excuses?

Many choose the latter.

Many choose the convalescent homes of the heart. Healthy bodies. Sharp minds. But retired dreams. Back and forth they rock in the chair of regret, repeating the terms of surrender. Lean closely and you will hear them: "If only." The white flag of the heart.

"If only . . ."

"If only I'd been born somewhere else . . ."

"If only I'd been treated fairly . . ."

"If only I'd had kinder parents, more money, greater opportunites . . ."

"If only I'd been potty-trained sooner, spanked less, or taught to eat without slurping."

Maybe you've used those words. Maybe you have every right to use them. Perhaps you, like Josiah, were hearing the ten count before you even got into the ring. For you to find an ancestor worth imitating, you, like Josiah, have to flip way back in your family album.

If such is the case, let me show you where to turn. Put down the scrapbook and pick up your Bible. Go to John's gospel and read Jesus' words: "Human life comes from human parents, but spiritual life comes from the Spirit" (John 3:6).

Think about that. Spiritual life comes from the Spirit! Your parents may have given you genes, but God gives you grace. Your parents may be responsible for your body, but God has taken charge of your soul. You may get your looks from your mother, but you get eternity from your Father, your heavenly Father.

By the way, He's not blind to your problems. In fact, God is willing to give you what your family didn't.

Didn't have a good father? He'll be your Father.

Through God you are a son; and, if you are a son, then you are certainly an heir. (Gal. 4:7 phillips)

Didn't have a good role model? Try God.

You are God's children whom he loves, so try to be like him. (Eph. 5:1)

Never had a parent who wiped away your tears? Think again. God has noted each one.

You have seen me tossing and turning through the night. You have collected all my tears in your bottle! You have recorded every one in your book. (Ps. 56:8 TLB)

God has not left you adrift on a sea of heredity. Just like Josiah, you cannot control the way your forefathers responded to God. But you can control the way *you* respond to Him. The past does not have to be your prison. You have a voice in your destiny. You have a say in your life. You have a choice in the path you take.

Choose well and someday—generations from now—your grandchildren and great-grandchildren will thank God for the seeds you sowed.

*Discussion Guide*
· · · · · · ·

## CHAPTER ONE
## GET RID OF REGRET

*Points to Ponder*

"Could it be that you went to religion and
didn't go to God? Could it be that you went
to a church, but never saw Christ?"

1    Have you ever gone to "religion" instead of
     God? If so, what happened?
2    How is it possible to go to church but not
     see Christ? Do you see Christ when you go
     to church? Explain.

"Go to Him. Be honest with Him. Admit
you have soul secrets you've never dealt
with. He already knows what they are. He's
just waiting for you to ask Him to help.
He's just waiting for you to give Him your
sack. Go ahead. You'll be glad you did."

1    How do you go to Jesus? Have you ever
     gone to Him like this?
2    Ask yourself what things are in your sack.
     Have you brought these things to Him? If
     not, why not?

*Wisdom from the Word*

≥   Read 2 Corinthians 7:5–13. What is the
    connection between sorrow and regret in
    this passage (see especially verse 10)? What
    does godly sorrow produce?
≥   Read Matthew 11:28–30. What does Jesus
    tell us to do in this passage? How do we do
    it? What is the result? Have you experienced
    such "rest"? Explain.

# CHAPTER TWO
## DEALING WITH ANGER

*Points to Ponder*

"When we are mistreated, our animalistic response is to go on the hunt. Instinctively we double up our fists. Getting even is only natural. Which, incidentally, is precisely the problem. Revenge is natural, not spiritual. Getting even is the rule of the jungle. Giving grace is the rule of the kingdom."

1   Does the "rule of the jungle" or the "rule of the kingdom" most often characterize your response to mistreatment?

2   Give an example of how you react to mistreatment.

"Revenge is irreverent. When we strike back we are saying, 'I know vengeance is Yours, God, but I just didn't think You'd punish enough. I thought I'd better take this situation into my own hands. You have a tendency to be a little soft.'"

1   Have you ever felt the way the paragraph above describes? Explain.

2   If you've ever acted out this feeling, what was the result?

"Forgiveness comes easier with a wide-angle lens. Joseph uses one to get the whole picture. He refuses to focus on the betrayal of his brothers without also seeing the loyalty of his God."

1   How does forgiveness come easier with a "wide-angle lens"?

2   How is it made more difficult with a "telephoto lens"?

*Wisdom from the Word*

ᴥ  Read Proverbs 20:22. What negative
    command is given here? What positive
    command is given? How do the two work
    together?

ᴥ  Read Genesis 50:15–21. Did Joseph have a
    right to be angry about the way his brothers
    mistreated him? How did he react? What
    was the result? If you were Joseph, how do
    you think you would have reacted?

## CHAPTER THREE
## THE FOUNDATION OF FAITH

*Points to Ponder*

"There is more to life than meets the eye.
For that's what faith is. Faith is trusting
what the eye can't see. Eyes see the prowling
lion. Faith sees Daniel's angel. Eyes see
storms. Faith sees Noah's rainbow. Eyes see
giants. Faith sees Canaan."

1  Do you agree that "faith is trusting what the
   eye can't see"?

2  Is there more to it than that? Explain.

"'I only jump to big arms.' If we think the
arms are weak, we won't jump. For that
reason, the Father flexed His muscles."

1  How has God demonstrated His "big arms"
   in your own life?

2  What's the biggest "arm flexing" you've ever
   experienced?

*Wisdom from the Word*

ᴥ  Read Hebrews 11:1–3. How is faith defined
    in this passage? How would you put this in
    your own words?

- Read Psalm 20. What lessons of trust do you learn from this passage? What promises are given? What hope is expressed?
- Read Ephesians 1:19–20. Does this passage help build your own faith? Explain. How does Paul use this passage in Ephesians?

## CHAPTER FOUR
## OVERCOMING YOUR HERITAGE

*Points to Ponder*

"We can't choose our parents, but we can choose our mentors."

1 What mentors have you chosen?
2 Why did you choose these particular individuals?

"Maybe your past isn't much to brag about. You saw raw evil. And now you, like Josiah, have to make a choice. Do you rise above the past and make a difference?

Or do you remain controlled by the past and make excuses?"

1 Choose one word to describe how you feel about your past: Grateful? Angry? Discouraged? Proud? Depressed? Blessed?
2 How do we sometimes allow ourselves to be controlled by the past? Have you ever slipped into this mode? Explain.

"Spiritual life comes from the Spirit! Your parents may have given you genes, but God gives you grace. Your parents may be responsible for your body, but God has taken charge of your soul. You may get your looks from your mother, but you get eternity from your Father, your heavenly Father."

1    How does this principle change our whole
     outlook?
2    What sort of spiritual heritage do you have
     now? Describe it.

*Wisdom from the Word*

* Read 2 Kings 21. Describe Josiah's heritage.
  How do you think he felt about it?

* Read John 3:1–8. How did Jesus explain
  that we can receive a spiritual heritage?
  What must we do? How did the Spirit move
  in your own life? Where did the "wind"
  come from?

* Read 2 Corinthians 5:17. What does it
  mean to be "in Christ"? What is gained?
  What is lost?